Lord Shaftesbury...

James Joseph Ellis

LORD SHAFTESBURY.

From a Photograph by Samuel A. Walker.

LORD SHAFTESBURY.

BY

REV. JAMES J. ELLIS

NEW YORK:
THOMAS WHITTAKER,
2 & 3 BIBLE HOUSE.

LORD SHAFTESBURY

LORD SHAFTESBURY.

BY

REV. JAMES J. ELLIS,

AUTHOR OF

"LORD LAWRENCE," "LORD WOLSELEY," ETC. ETC.

" Austere he was not ; yet the pompous joys
Of life to him seemed sadly unavailing.
His kings, unsceptred, were but lonely boys
Across the ocean sailing.
He lived a gentle Christian knight,
And died a martyr to imperious duty."

NEW YORK:

THOMAS WHITTAKER,

2 & 3 BIBLE HOUSE.

210636

PREFACE.

——+——

THE name of Lord Shaftesbury has long been a synonym for unwearied and wide-reaching philanthropy, begun in a spirit familiar, indeed, to those who have studied the career of Howard and those like him, but which excites surprise on account of the magnitude of its aims and the vastness of its operations. For while it has been the honour of many that they have laboured with a steady resolution, no one has been able to enlist so many helpers, grasp so many differing enterprises, and compel them all to serve together for the one object in view as did Lord Shaftesbury.

There seems, indeed, no branch of philanthropy which he did not to some extent acquire and assist; no good doing within reach which he did not hasten to study, encourage, and as far as in him lay to imitate. Thus, a list of the institutions of which he was president or vice-president, or an interested co-worker, would exhaust the various societies that are the glory of this century. Lord Shaftesbury came thus into contact with Churchmen, Dissenters, and Romanists; and with a catholicity which is a mark of a spirit at one with God, he laboured with all who sought to serve Christ, even with differences of operation that he disliked. No matter if they held opinions that he strongly disapproved and was even ready to combat; if he thought they were sincerely labouring for the social benefit of their fellows, his hand was ready to greet and cheer them in the path he could not altogether tread in their society. Inured himself to dispense with sympathy, he was eager to give it to them, and all the more if the recipients were workers with but few encouragements, as were Orsman and Holland.

The influence of his life is eternal, and the facts of his career are a moral music to which many feet will keep time in their march through the desert on to the city of God. To live as he lived, to work from the same motives that impelled him to constant assiduity such as men generally reserve for the pursuit of wealth and fame; above all, to be prepared to sacrifice all that impedes the attainment of the mission entrusted to our care, ought to be the resolve of all in this nineteenth century of grace who have been even indirectly benefited by him.

For the influence of good men, like the perfume of a field of lavender, travels far and lingers long; and there is no man now living who has not been assisted in a thousand ways by the reforms that Lord Shaftesbury devised, assisted, or perfected.

> " Let us do our work as well,
>   Both the unseen and the seen."

HARRINGAY, LONDON, N.,
  March 1892.

CONTENTS.

——

CHAPTER I.

1801–1828.

NOT ORPHANED, BUT MOTHERLESS.

CHAPTER II.

1828–1840.

AT THE CRY OF NEED; THE FRIEND OF THE HELPLESS.

CHAPTER III.

1840-1842.

THE WORKING MAN'S FRIEND.

CHAPTER IV.

1843-1850.

FRESH LABOUR ADDED TO OLD SINEWS.

CHAPTER V.

1851-1863.

"THAT'S OUR LORD SHAFTESBURY."

CHAPTER VI.

1864–1881.

KNIGHT OF THE GARTER AND COSTER.

CHAPTER VII.

1881–1885.

"EVEN SO, COME, LORD JESUS!"

EARL SHAFTESBURY.

CHAPTER I.

NOT ORPHANED, BUT MOTHERLESS.

"Pity the sorrows of a poor young child ;
No mother's love on him has smiled."—PAYNE.

"There is no overdone earnestness ; life is not crushed out of us by the sledge-hammer of the statistical bore ; there is the charm of disengagement, and the faculty of disengagement is one of the secrets of the most effective kind of character."—COBDEN.

1801–1828.

KNOCKING DOWN THE NAIL—THE LANGUAGE OF CONDUCT—ONLY A NURSE, BUT A TRUE NURSE—THE CALL OF GOD TO HIS WORK—A NARROW ESCAPE—IN THE RIGHT PLACE TO DO HIS BEST—WISELY USING TIME IN MOSAIC—"FOLLOWING HIM WHO GUIDES ME"—IN TRUST FOR OTHERS.

MARY HOWITT, in her charming autobiography, informs us that while in Germany she observed a nail, two inches in length, projecting from the plank by which intending passengers passed from the shore to the boat. One after another stumbled against the nail

A

and injured themselves or their garments, until at
length there came a man who ordered the nail to
be driven into the board. "Sir, forgive my freedom," said a man who stood by, "but that simple
fact shows me that you are an Englishman." Perhaps the opinion is somewhat too favourable for our
national pride, but the natives of these isles are
certainly prompt enough in removing that which
inconveniences them, unless, of course, they are paid
to allow the nails to remain in the plank. To clear
out of the path of the friendless and the feeble that
which might hinder or harm them; to render their
pathway along the slippery plank as safe as it can
possibly be; to be himself hurt by the nails he ex-
tracted, was the mission of Lord Shaftesbury, whose
life-story is not only part of our national history,
but a chronicle of the triumph of the Gospel of God.

A painter once said, "I speak no language but
German and *that*," pointing to his last picture.
The language of behaviour, of achievement, and of
temptation resisted is the noblest speech that any
hero can utter. Lord Shaftesbury's linguistic abilities are of no interest now, save as a proof of his
industry and native ability, but the language of his
life is still truth set to music, and that to every
class.

He was born to a title and such fame as ancestors
who have been eminent in the state can transmit
to their descendants, but he was not born to that
love which alone renders life beautiful, useful, and

honourable to God. His father, Cropley, the sixth Earl of Shaftesbury, was able, busy, and doubtless well-meaning according to his lights, but he was much occupied by the duties of his parliamentary position, and but little disposed naturally to waste time in those endearments that, trifling as they appear, are the most powerful educational forces of childhood. The sense of interest, the joy of being trusted and loved, awaken the noblest purposes, and prepare a child to receive without mental irritation other commands, the reasons of which are not at the time perceived. Even if some allowance may be made for the Earl, none can be made for the mother of the boy, who, not knowing that her sole title to honour would be her relationship to the son born at 24 Grosvenor Square on the 28th of April 1801, had no higher care or purpose in life than to please herself, to spend in the frivolities of fashion the abilities which no one receives for selfish or merely personal uses.

It was a case of the ostrich nurture; but fortunately not the sand, but the fostering care of a stranger had been provided by Almighty God, who always compensates for what He permits any life to lack.

"It is surely a fact worth noting," says the author of the "Life of Archbishop Tait," "that three at least among the leading public men of our generation, Lord Shaftesbury, Lord Lawrence, and Archbishop Tait, have each of them, on recalling the

main influence which contributed to mould their
lives, assigned a foremost place to the nurse of
their early years." One Maria Mills, who had been
his mother's maid, and was now her housekeeper,
without knowing that she was creating an age-
saviour and training a great teacher and leader,
taught the loveless boy, gave young Ashley affection,
and, what was even better still, a knowledge of, and
a relish for, the truths of the Gospel as she knew
them. Only until he was seven years of age was her
ministry continued, but during that brief interval
she awoke his soul, turned it Godwards, and led him
to love the Bible and the Christ of whom the Bible
speaks. She had given a twist to his being that it
never afterwards lost. To his dying day the Earl
wore the watch that she gave him, and to his dying
day he offered the prayer that she taught his youth-
ful lips to utter. So may it be ours to prevent a
soul from injuring others, and mould it by the truth
we teach for the noblest ends and destiny.

At the age of seven the boy left this nurse for a
school at Chiswick, which proved to be a school of
the rod-and-wickedness type. The ostrich nurture
was succeeded by that which was like training for
the infernal pit. The memory and influence not
only of Maria Mills, but of the Greater Teacher, with
whom she had made the boy acquainted, enabled
him to endure the school, and at holiday-time even
the home where the children were less regarded
than was the furniture.

Relief came at last, when young Ashley was sent to Harrow at the age of twelve years. Not that Harrow was Paradise, but it was better than Chiswick, and, sad to relate, it was better than what was called home, which latter place was only a house containing furniture and human beings who were as irresponsive as were the tables and chairs. At Harrow, one of the masters, being unable to sleep, would provide himself companions in misfortune by calling up poor sleepy boys at four o'clock on a winter's morning for such lessons as they could learn under circumstances so unfavourable! The boy had endured worse, and probably did not so much heed school troubles, because they were in his view inevitable and inseparable from such a life.

At Harrow, when fourteen years of age, an event occurred which, acting upon the character formed by Maria Mills, fixed his destiny. For events act upon us according to our mental or moral condition, just as a mould will fix its imprint upon molten, but leave cold iron unmarked. The incident was common enough, and had been seen by many before without exciting more than disgust. Some drunken men, who were carrying one of their companions to the grave, dropped their burden and gave vent to the foul speech which is the natural expression of a wicked heart. The youth saw more than the incidents of the tragedy, he heard more than the foul curses of the men. He saw an example of everyday and widespread ignorance; he heard, too, the

voice of God calling him to do his duty to enlighten
as he had been enlightened, and he resolved to do
what he might.

Mrs. Sewell called her father " an enthusiast held
in the fetters of circumstances ; " henceforward Lord
Ashley was an enthusiast unfettered, and this is
possible for all who desire so to be. Many an
enthusiast is fettered by the love of money, dread
of trouble, or by sheer laziness. Rise and break what-
ever hinders or limits thy doing all that is possible
with thy talents for the relief of the sorrow that now
calls without response from thee. " Bill," said a
rough sailor, " I can't stand that look upon your
face," and he plunged into the sea to rescue his
sinking friend. Lord Ashley saw the look of appeal,
and replied to it ; henceforward his life had an end
in view, towards which it employed all its strength
and skill in a continuous strain.

At Oxford Lord Ashley took honours, success
which was not at all to the surprise of those who
had watched his diligence and persistence in study.
He entered Parliament in due course, as a young
man of twenty-five in those times might have been
expected to do. He took the oaths on the 16th of
November 1826 as member for Woodstock. The Earl
had some thoughts at one time of placing his son in
the army, but a Wiser than he had ordered otherwise. Only in Parliament could Lord Ashley fulfil
the mission entrusted to his care. The Duke of
Wellington was, singularly enough, attracted by the

young man, and although he had but little sympathy with Lord Ashley's philanthropy, the Duke
continued the friendship all through his life.

Two sentences comprise what is perhaps as accurate an account of Lord Ashley's hopes and intentions
in entering the political arena as any that can be
given. "I want nothing but usefulness to God
and my country," said he; "I had rather be creep-
ing and contented than aspiring and inefficient." A
young man animated by such unselfish desire of
thoroughness in service must always become happy
in himself and helpful to others.

On the 18th of April 1827 a place in the
Ministry was offered to him by Canning. Although
the offer was not accepted, the fact that it was
made at all is a proof of the esteem in which the
young man was held by those who were accus-
tomed to weigh and measure men. Lord Ashley
gave a remarkable proof of his intellectual abilities
in the September of the same year by mastering
the Welsh language, a tongue of which Paxton
Hood said, "Its words start before the eye like pic-
tures, but are conveyed to the mind like music;
and yet the very character of the language adds to
the picture dramatic action and living strength."

The first official position that Lord Ashley held
was a Commissionership of the India Board of
Control, which was conferred upon him, on the
29th of January 1828, by his friend the Duke of
Wellington. This post, which he held for two

years, was of great importance to him in a pecuniary
sense ; for the Earl, his father, carried his harshness
to the point of limiting the amount paid to his
children to what was far below the income they
might reasonably have anticipated from his wealth
and resources.   As was becoming in a young man
who had to employ his office for the purposes it
was intended to accomplish rather than merely to
reap its fruits, Lord Ashley gave himself to a
diligent study of the needs of the people committed
to his care.   Hence, unlike the majority of his
contemporaries, he had an intelligent interest in the
great dependency he ruled, because he realised its
needs and claims.

In Parliament he had not as yet made any mark ;
for nearly two years he was an all but silent
member.   But during all that time he was dili-
gently preparing himself for the as yet unrealised
service awaiting him.   Such is the wisdom of God,
that those who acquire fitness in due time invariably
make a sphere for the exercise of that ability which
is less native than acquired ; for we are largely
what we make ourselves, and that we become in
spite of the influence or opposition of others.   Of
his chosen and congenial vocation, Disraeli said
that a statesman's life was " the only career in
which a man is never old ; " " for," he said, " a
statesman can feel and inspire interest longer than
any other man."   Which, of course, must be taken
with due allowances, and yet is not wholly untrue.

Be this as it may, a statesman's life Lord Ashley had selected, and he strove to fulfil his duty. Among other improvements for the well-being of the Indian races to which Lord Ashley gave attention was a design to found a society to encourage horticulture and scientific husbandry, in place of the surface scratching which the ancients termed tilling the soil. The missionaries at Serampore had done much in this direction; for Carey and his associates were educators of the highest order.

Lord Ashley's tasks were not always so pleasant as this project for the Indian people; for, sincerely Protestant as he was, after the type now, alas! very rare, Lord Ashley was called upon, in common with many of his party who felt as he did, to make a departure which they regarded as perilous. The plots and intrigues of the Romanists under Elizabeth and James had necessitated severe and repressive laws against them. These were directed against them, not as members of an alien Church, but as the subjects and spies of a foreign enemy. The behaviour of Romanists under James II. did not lessen the public dread of their plots, but, with the firm establishment of the House of Hanover, many Protestants felt that laws justifiable enough at one time might be dispensed with, or at least relaxed. Precautions that may be wise when garrotters abound are not required when the law has rendered outrage impossible or unlikely.

Sir Robert Peel, therefore, introduced a measure

for the purpose of releasing Romanists from the
state of alienation and practical outlawry in which
they had lived.   With the House of Commons but
little difficulty was expected, but men wondered
how the Duke of Wellington would be able to
induce the House of Lords to assent to the measure.
Lord Clarendon said, " Oh, that will be easy enough.
He'll say, ' My Lords!   Attention!   Right about
face!   March!'"   Which in effect he did, and was
obeyed.

During the leisure moments that many waste,
but which if well employed are the richest seed-plots
of life, Lord Ashley learned Hebrew, a tongue he
loved because of his reverence for the Holy Scriptures.   Like all who have tasted of the vintage, he
desired to press the grapes for himself—to get at
the original without the intervention of translator
or translation.

With infinite scorn, Disraeli said that Sir Robert
Peel's life was " one great appropriation clause."
Every life in one sense must appropriate if it would
impart that which other lives will value.   Some,
indeed, appropriate that which is harmful, for the
tree of knowledge has some poisonous as well as
some bitter fruits ; others annex merely rubbish ;
they are collectors of odds and ends not worth
the cost and trouble involved in gathering them.
That which healthily instructs, makes nobler, and
renders the possessor more capable of self-sacrifice for others, that alone is worth appropriating.

And that we may take them, God only hides partially the gifts and treasures of His wisdom and love. Clive wondered at his own moderation in taking so little when he might have taken vastly greater wealth; we may well say the same. Lord Ashley appropriated knowledge at every possible chance, and it seemed at one time as if it would be his function to serve as a student of science, a ministry of the noblest function and with benefits of priceless value to confer upon men. To his well-ordered mind the laws that govern life, and the limitless riches into which discovery can only bore a little way, presented great attraction. As an expositor of the wilderness of ordered but tangled thought that we call science, Lord Ashley would have been eminent had he followed his liking and bent. For as Kepler, after twenty years of study, exclaimed when he detected the relation of the planets, "Oh, Almighty God, I think Thy thoughts after Thee," it is the work of the scientist to think God's thoughts, and under their influence to quicken other minds into thought and activity. This was not to be Lord Ashley's aim; another and equally important service awaited him, and in order to equip and devote himself fully to it, he cast off even that which pleased him best.

There was, indeed, need for a reformer, and of a type never before seen. The long war had left a legacy of savagery and of degradation which no effort had been able to adequately deal with; it seemed, indeed, immense, and utterly beyond all hope of amelioration. Religion was utterly unknown to a large number of the natives of these isles; the means of life were difficult to obtain, at least by those who were honest, while bands of criminals throve in vice for a brief time, and then died without dread because ignorant of the judgment to come. To deal with first one form of evil and of suffering, and then another; to devise one method of alleviation after another; to struggle long, and at the cost of personal health and reputation, for the smallest success, was the life-work of Lord Shaftesbury, or, as he was then called, Lord Ashley. Not that at the commencement of his career he probably realised a tithe of the service to be demanded from him, but, like a good soldier, he obeyed the commands as they came. Of his life-work Constantine's words are true in every sense, as they may also be true of our lives. When, in 328, the Emperor marked out the site that his new city called Constantinople was to occupy, his courtiers wondered at the magnitude of the area he was enclosing. The Emperor replied, "I am following Him who is leading me," a phrase that, upon his lips, was an empty vaunt. But it is true of all who will follow in all things the guiding providences which indicate our duty, sometimes dimly, sometimes with terrible clearness; for such will ever find that a life so mapped out will attain a magnitude and majesty impossible to others. One man marks out his life thus: " So much wealth, which means so much pleasure, which in turn brings so much credit, to the glory and praise of myself." Another, like Lord Ashley, seeks to do the right, and is amazed to find that God has added pleasure, and perhaps honour, thereunto. No wiser words can be spoken by any man than those uttered by Prince Albert, who said to those who were his juniors, "Find out the plan of God in your day, and then beware that you do not cross it, but fall into your own place in that plan."

Lord Ashley did this, and so may we, and then it will be possible for us to live nobly and with infinite profit to those who, for their good or harm, share the world with us in our day and generation.

That they are companions of our service is in some sense to make us responsible for their wise and noble behaviour; for every man in his degree is put in trust with regard to his generation, which may be helped or hindered by him and his doings.

> " To serve the present age,
>   My calling to fulfil,
> Oh, may it all my powers engage
>   To do my Master's will."

CHAPTER II.

AT THE CRY OF NEED; THE FRIEND OF THE HELPLESS.

" His heart was pure and simple as a child's,
Unbreathed on by the world; in friendship warm,
Confiding, generous, constant; and now
He ranks among the great ones of the earth,
And hath achieved such glory as will last
To future generations."—MOULTRIE.

"In the person of Lord Shaftesbury we have an example of one who has fulfilled so many missions, that some of them are hardly remembered by the present generation."—G. H. PIKE.

1828–1840.

FACING THE FACTS—KINDNESS TO THE UNKIND—WHITE SLAVES AND THEIR TYRANTS—IN THE PILLORY—"GO FORWARD AND TO VICTORY"—CHILDREN WITHOUT PLAY —AN ICEBERG UNTHAWED—CHICKEN-STEALERS IN ALARM —NOT A GARMENT, BUT A LIFE—RECONCILED TO HIS FATHER—A HOUSE WORTH VISITING.

THE call of the wounded on the battlefield of Borodino for help is said to have been like the roar of the sea—a terrible agony of sorrow, crying for succour that, alas! did not come. Such a sound Lord Ashley heard, and at once did what lay within his power to afford assistance to the wounded and dying. The many deplorable sufferers who had lost their reason—then treated like beasts—first claimed his attention. Our forefathers generally regarded the insane as inspired; but sometimes they believed the inspiration to be of God, and therefore to be accepted; at other times, and generally, of Satan, and to be beaten out of the sufferer. The recital of the wrongs of poor creatures already sufficiently punished by the deprivation of reason is appalling. A great novelist has made it the theme of one of his most sensational but truthful stories, and perhaps therein he rendered the greatest service of his life in awaking the public to a sense of the terrible evils endured by many who were also unable to plead their own cause. For a great philosopher has said that the active life of man is an attempt to forget the facts of his own existence. Lord Ashley faced the facts and endeavoured to alter them. His first speech of any length in Parliament was delivered on the 19th of February 1828, when he pleaded on behalf of the lunatics. When the Bill he then supported became law on the 15th of July 1828, he was appointed Chairman of the Commissioners to whom the charge of the insane was then entrusted. For nearly sixty years Lord Ashley held this post; it was an office which entailed a large amount of unpaid labour, besides involving much personal inconvenience. He himself visited the places where the lunatics were confined; he saw

with his own eyes the treatment to which they
were subjected, and this gave a reality to his pleas
on their behalf that made his words authoritative.
He confessed that "there was nothing poetical" in
his duty, but he merely consoled himself with the
reflection that "every sigh prevented and every
pang subdued is a song of harmony to the heart;"
or, as Herbert said when he performed a deed of
kindness, "these are things that set the bells of
the heart ringing." We have a portrait of Lord
Ashley at this period of his life sketched by the
late Earl Granville, who at the Mansion House
meeting in 1884 said: "He was then a singularly
good-looking man, with absolutely nothing of effemi-
nate beauty. He had those manly good looks and
that striking presence which, I believe—though, of
course, inferior by hundreds of degrees to the graces
of mind and character—help a man more than we
sometimes think, and they helped him when he
endeavoured to inspire his humble fellow-country-
men with his noble and elevated nature." Lord
Ashley had indeed need of every advantage, for
to labour already more than sufficient to fully
occupy his mind, like every busy man, he found
time to add other employments that were even
more engrossing.

The introduction of machinery into the manufacture of cotton goods had immensely developed
their production, with, of course, the attendant evils
incident to prosperity. Instead of working at home

as of old, workers were now gathered into huge factories, where child-labour became almost as profitable as that of adults; the former also was easily attainable. The workhouses of London and other great cities were swept of their poor children, who were sent in waggons or in barges to their destination. A class of men made it their business to scour the country in order to buy children for service in the factories. The demand for these white slaves was so keen, that one manufacturer actually permitted one idiot to be thrown in with every score of perfect children.

Beside the factory stood the apprentice-house, the beds in which were not permitted to grow cool, for the machinery being kept going both night and day, the beds were occupied in succession by the apprentices. Mr. Sadler, at one time Member for Newark, had attempted to arouse Parliament to a sense of the misery and degradation of these children. He at length found himself outside the House of Commons, and cast about to secure some one to take up the cause in which he had interested himself. He soon found the right man. On the 6th of February 1833 Lord Ashley undertook the task.

Among the wonders of Marseilles Museum is a painting known as *Le Pilori*. In this great picture most of the great men who have taught and helped their fellow-creatures, and suffered for their good deeds, are represented, and beneath all is the inscription—

B

"They are persecuted ;
They are hidden in oblivion ;
Until, after a long time elapses,
They have a monument inscribed,
TO THE GLORY OF THE HUMAN RACE."

The great undertaking Lord Shaftesbury assumed
placed him in the pillory, and that for a long time.
The most painful experience of all his long-con-
tinued obloquy must have been the opposition (and
worse) of men like Bright and Gladstone, who are
wholly estimable in themselves, but who disliked
Lord Ashley and resisted his labours.   Medical
men, too, were found who were not ashamed to
declare that factory children required no recreation
at all.   "Do you think it would benefit a child's
health of eight years to be kept twelve hours upon
his legs ?" was a question asked of one of these
doctors.   He replied, "Really, I am not prepared
to answer that question."   The Bishop of Autun
once said, "Mazarin never told lies, but always
deceived you ; now Metternich always tells lies,
but never deceives you."   The sycophant doctors
did not deceive any except those who were anxious
to be deceived.

Lord Ashley counted well the cost of the course
he had selected for himself ; he knew well that the
Duke of Wellington and others, from whose favour
he might reasonably expect honour and office, would
forsake him if he meddled in matters they were
content to ignore ; but he ran the risk and paid the

price exacted. His noble wife encouraged him to undertake the duty and leave the consequences to God. "Go forward," said she, "and to victory." And he went forward, and after a time won.

The Reform Bill had brought a great many manufacturers into Parliament without giving the franchise to those who suffered from the factory evils. Looking to the supposed necessity of sustaining themselves in office by the votes of the wealthy mill-owners and their connections, one Government after another deferred the question of relieving the operatives until indeed it could be no longer safely delayed. To the national shame be it said, that it required twenty years of persistent pleading and effort before it was rendered illegal to employ children of tender years and others more than ten and a half hours per day.

The mill-owners, looking naturally to their profits, and equally naturally not seeing the evils only too evident to those who suffered from them, urged and obtained a Commission to inquire into the alleged grievances. This device, it is true, delayed, but it also had a result its originators little expected, for it more clearly demonstrated the urgent need that there was for redress. At Manchester, and again at Leeds, the miserable factory children as they left their toilsome employment were paraded before the Commissioners, who were thus able to see for themselves the physical evils that were complained of.

On the 17th of June 1833 Lord Ashley introduced a Bill, the purpose of which was to limit the
working-day for factory children to ten hours.
This measure was opposed by the Government
(although more than 200,000 persons petitioned
in its favour) and rejected.   The Government introduced a Bill of their own, which provided, after a
lapse of three years, that children under nine were
not to be employed in any but silk and lace mills,
and those under thirteen were not to be confined
more than forty-eight hours per week.   Two hours
schooling per week was also ordered; but the Bill
remained inoperative owing to the opposition of the
magistrates, many of whom were mill-owners, and
therefore opposed to legislation, the necessity of
which they naturally could not perceive.   Satisfied
that no more could be effected for the present,
Lord Ashley, with his wife and child, left London
for a six months' tour through the Continent,
watching every one, and seeing all with an eye to
the moral bearing of everything; thus spending his
time, he gathered not only physical strength, but
mental and spiritual vigour, which he freely spent
for the service of the needy during this holiday.

Lord and Lady Ashley reached England in
May 1834, almost immediately after William IV.
had pettishly dismissed his Ministers.   Sir Robert
Peel, although not responsible for this stretch of
prerogative, did not refuse to accept the office thus
vacant, and somewhat reluctantly Lord Ashley con-

sented to become one of the Lords of the Admiralty. He took a lower office than he might justly have secured had he pushed his claims to place and power, and on the 13th of January 1835 was re-elected to Parliament after his appointment without any opposition. But he was not to hold office long, for on the 8th of April of the same year Lord John Russell defeated the Ministry, and Lord Melbourne once more succeeded to power, which he held until the fourth year of the present reign.

The following year, 1836, is chiefly memorable in Lord Ashley's history for the formation of the Church Pastoral Aid Society, which was organised to provide lay helpers, then almost unknown, for such clergymen as desired what is now recognised as indispensable; and in March of the same year the Government, who had been compelled to yield some protection to children under thirteen years of age, withdrew from their pledge. Mr. Paulett Thompson, in their name, declared that sixty-nine hours per week was not too much for such children, and threatened that unless his Bill were carried, all the children, numbering some thirty-five thousand, would be dismissed from their employment. Lord Ashley, undeterred by this threat, which was no empty vaunt, led the opposition with such success, that the Ministry only obtained a majority of two for their Bill, which they wisely abandoned.

Convinced now that the slight conquest already

made could only be retained by a vigorous aggression, Lord Ashley returned once and again to what appeared a hopeless attack.

On the 20th of July 1838 he again brought the case before the House of Commons, and pleaded for an amendment of the existing law. He proved that in some of the mills little children travelled twenty or thirty miles per day up and down amidst whirling machinery, in dust and an atmosphere reeking with oil and grease. So terrible was the strain upon the physical powers this protracted toil involved, that quite apart from those who were injured by falling on the machinery or being caught in it, more persons died under twenty in the factory districts than under forty in other parts of the kingdom. Manchester had the bad pre-eminence in this respect, for half the number of its population died under the age of three years.

The moral and social degradation of the poor creatures was such as might have been expected from such conditions. Whittaker, ex-Mayor of Scarborough, who himself was a factory-boy in his early years, has left us a picture of the homes and habits of his associates, which, to say the least of it, is deplorable.

These facts, lamentable as they were, made no impression upon the House of Commons, who were under the fear of the mill-owners. Factory masters, who would not, and county squires, who could not, understand the feelings of the factory operatives, were unlikely to consent to the alteration demanded. They had none of them the training that Lord Ashley had received, for none of them had seen with their own eyes the evils by means of which some of them had acquired wealth and position. Had they done so, some of them at least would have attempted a reform of some of the most flagrant abuses.

In May 1839 Lord Ashley ran a narrow risk of sinking into a court official. Lord Melbourne, who had come into conflict with the planters of Jamaica, resolved to deprive them of the authority they had abused. He was, however, defeated in the Commons and resigned office. Sir Robert Peel attempted to form a Ministry, but failed through a misunderstanding. " Peel has no manners," said the Duke of Wellington, and he might have added that Peel unfortunately had the atmosphere of an iceberg. In Sir Robert Peel the national hauteur was yet more frigid perhaps from policy. He failed to make allowance for the warm feelings with which the Queen regarded her friends, and Lord Melbourne resumed office. Had Peel been successful, he had selected Lord Ashley for a post in the Royal Household, alleging the need that there was for placing those about the Queen who would influence her in the right way. Lord Ashley, unwilling as he was to abandon his own particular work, said that if by consenting to Peel's request he could help the Queen and country, he would willingly become chief scullion in her kitchen. Peel probably under-

stood the wisdom of placing so independent, and,
worst of all, so earnest a follower where he could not
disturb mill-owners, whose votes were required, but
who felt, when Lord Ashley spoke, as did the negro
congregation when their minister preached upon
the sin of chicken-stealing—that is, uncomfortable,
resentful, and not at all profited by the discourse.

Chicken-stealers are all alike, and we must not
judge them too harshly when we remember that Lord
Ashley himself opposed many wise and needful reforms. Brought up amidst influences that were not of
the best, this is not to be wondered at. Lord Ashley
was only like his opponents, who failed to approve
of the remedial measures introduced by another.
He himself was indeed a good hater, and indulged
this propensity to the utmost. One is not surprised,
for example, that the Duke of Wellington opposed
the new Board of Education devised by Lord Russell.
To the Iron Duke all the poorer classes were so
many herds to be taxed, ruled, fed, and kept quiet.
He failed to realise that in every human breast
there beats a soul for which Christ died and which
may live in His heaven. But it is pitiful that
Lord Ashley should resist the formation of the
authority which has done so much to wipe out the
disgraceful ignorance that, as Kingsley has pointed
out, is the parent of much of the vice and misery
once prevailing among us. Very perplexing it is,
and quite incapable of adequate explanation, that
men like Bright, Cobden, and Ashley should have

so little understood and appreciated each others'
motives and labours.   Each saw a need and laboured
to supply it, but neither of them understood that
all together were working out the great purpose and
plan of God.

In August 1839 Lord Ashley went to Scotland,
and on the way visited Robert Southey the poet.
There was much likeness between the two noble
men, and for years they were co-workers together
for the relief of the poor, the young, and the de-
fenceless.

For Scotland Lord Ashley had the liking that all
Englishmen who have visited it acquire; he saw its
faults; he did not agree with its theology, but he
admired the solid integrity which, more than anything
else, has made Scotchmen prominent in our national
annals.   Yet, amidst the pleasures of a round of
hospitalities, his philanthropy led him to observe the
methods by which Scotchmen sought to alleviate
the visitations of Providence and the effects of the
wrong-doing of humanity.

Of him might be said with perfect truth what
Lady Edwardes said of her husband, "He had
always a heart to sympathise and a hand to stretch
out to every one in trouble, and many were the
prayers that went up to bless him."   And with
equal truth may we quote a second time from the
same writer, saying of Lord Ashley as of General
Edwardes, "His life was his religion, which with him
was not a garment put on and worn on Sundays

and saints' days and great occasions, but the per-
meating influence of every action." As was seen
when he was in Scotland; for his diary abounds
in religious reflections that are characterised by
great spiritual insight and equally remarkable
felicity of expression. A religion that is not put
away during a holiday is, to say the least, probably
real.

Lord Ashley, too, was always eager for explana-
tions and proofs which every land supplies of the
Book, and that because he regarded the Bible as
the very Word of God.

Towards the end of this same year of 1839 Lord
Ashley was reconciled to his father, who invited him
to St. Giles, the ancestral home. At this time Lord
Ashley's family consisted of six children, who were
with him at St. Giles. Here perhaps will be the
most fitting place to speak of St. Giles, which is a
remarkable structure in itself, and also interesting
for its historical associations.

The first of the Ashleys who won fame was one
Antony Ashley, who was knighted by Queen Elizabeth for his bravery at the siege of Cadiz. In
Dorsetshire a tradition still lingers that he first
introduced the cabbage into England, but it is
believed that the legend is a popular attempt to
account for a ball of granite enclosed in a gilded
netting which lies on his tomb. The grandson
of this knight became the first Earl; he was the
man whom Charles II. pronounced " the wickedest

man in my dominions," and of whom the same King
said that he was " master of more law than all his
judges, and possessed of more divinity than all his
bishops."   An able, unscrupulous, licentious, restless man, who changed sides as his interests or
wishes prompted, but who on the whole rendered
somewhat unwilling service to the cause of liberty,
while he gratified his own desire for revenge.   A
huge beer-cask, in which four men might make their
abode, is preserved in St. Giles as a memorial of
this worthy; and on a board in the servants' hall
beneath the Royal Arms are the following rules,
which deserve attention.   They were written in his
time, if not by him :—

Prophane	no	Divine ordinance.
Touch	no	State matters.
Urge	no	Healths.
Pick	no	Quarrels.
Maintain	no	Ill opinions.
Encourage	no	Vice.
Repeat	no	Grievances.
Reveal	no	Secrets.
Make	no	Comparisons.
Keep	no	Bad company.
Make	no	Long meals.
Lay	no	Wagers.

These rules observed will obtain
Thy peace and everlasting gain.

St. Giles' House is almost a parallelogram, and
covers a considerable quantity of ground.   It stands
well among trees, which set off its beauties and

make it appear as stately as it is solid. The park is nine miles in circumference. In the entrance hall there is a huge black-jack of considerable antiquity, the little round rickety table upon which Thomson wrote "The Seasons," and the portrait of a Dorsetshire worthy who is famous, first, because he used the pulpit of his private chapel as a larder, and secondly, because he ate oysters twice a day every day in the year.

Beyond the entrance lies the Stone Hall, in which stands the bust of the seventh Earl, which was presented by the Lancashire operatives to Lady Shaftesbury. The house itself abounds in remarkable Chippendale furniture, and indeed contains some masterpieces of that artist.

At the western end of the pile, the room that Lord Ashley occupied when he succeeded to the estates remains just as it was in his day. The ugly green paper on the walls is covered with the many addresses he received from ragged-schools and other philanthropic institutions in which he took interest. Illuminated addresses in cases occupy the table, which is still covered by a cheap cloth, while more touching memorials occupy every available inch of space; such as some woollen mats worked by a poor widow, a marked pocket-handkerchief sent him by a child, a feeble attempt at modelling by which a cripple showed his love, and the patchwork quilt (beneath which the Earl slept) which was worked for him by some little girls who had been rescued by the Ragged School Union from unmentionable infamy. In the justice-room, which is contiguous, is the barrow which was given to the Earl by the costermongers of London. The walls of this room also are decorated with addresses and engravings of Homes that he founded. In this room it is said his farm-hands once imparted to him their desire to possess " a little holdin' for theirzelves." The Earl listened to all that was said, and quietly asked how the requisite capital for stocking the proposed farmstead was to be provided. " Well, my Lord, we would borrer zome o' you for't," said one farmer.

Among the out-buildings is a hothouse which was erected by the seventh Earl in memory of his wife, so that the flowers she loved might be continually reared.

On the south-eastern side of the house, canopied by large trees, stands a grotto which, during the seven years of its erection, cost the fourth Countess a sum amounting to £10,000. It consists of two caverns, the outer of which represents a cave under the sea, rich with crystals and coral which hang from the ceiling and line the walls. The inner chamber is yet more curious, for small shells are embedded in cement which is moulded to represent the irregular surface of a rock.

CHAPTER III.

THE WORKING MAN'S FRIEND.

" Rare gifts
Marked him for great things
In peace and war."

" How grand, how glorious a piece of handiwork he was ! It was a pleasure to behold him even ! And then his nature so fully equal to his form ! "—EDWARDES ON NICHOLSON.

1840–1842.

"HOW'S THE OLD COMPLAINT ?"—TO BE MARRIED IS TO BE
MANAGED—"BE YOU A PETER TAVEY MAN ?"—HOW TO
LEAD—"GIVE ME TIME"—THE JEWS AND PALESTINE—
THE VICTIM OF SAUNTERING — WANTED BACKBONES—
PAYING FOR HIS PRINCIPLES—IN THE RIGHT *VERSUS* IN
THE TREASURY—BEAR WHAT CANNOT BE MENDED.

MR. DISRAELI once said that if he met a man whose name he could not remember, he paused and said, " Ah ! how is the old complaint ? "—a custom based upon an accurate knowledge of human nature and the facts of life, for there is always an old complaint troubling individuals and people. The old complaint was to perplex and trouble Lord Ashley during the eventful year of 1840, which marks a distinct epoch

30

in our national story. In addition to his many ordinary labours, he then undertook and accomplished a fresh reform, which was in itself well worth doing, and which alone would constitute a claim on his behalf to high praise. In this year the Penny Postal system first came into operation, an experiment which has been attended with civilising influences of the highest importance. Cromwell told George Fox that if they were oftener together they would understand each other better, which is true of all men. Cheap railways, and indeed everything that facilitates intercourse, destroys the misunderstandings that are apt to engender bitterness and produce strife.

A few weeks before this important advance an event as interesting took place in the Chapel Royal, St. James's. The Queen on the 10th of February was married to her cousin Prince Albert, a man whose beneficial influence upon the national life was not acknowledged till after his death. Mr. Disraeli said that " to be married is to be managed." Prince Albert, on the contrary, managed England, and for the national benefit.

Lord and Lady Ashley were present at the wedding by invitation, the former with a keen appreciation of the character of the Queen, whom he had already learned to admire and love for her own graces and gifts.

On the 10th of June the Queen's life was attempted for the first time ; on that day a potboy, greedy of notoriety and crazy from reading bad books, fired at her. Lord Ashley understood the full peril to which the nation as well as the Queen had been exposed. Had she been killed, the detested King of Hanover would have come to the throne, with almost certain destruction to the monarchy. A man of whom the Duke of Wellington said that he loved to set friends at variance, who took wicked delight in making strife, and who to the manners of a bear linked the morals of a savage, could not but be repulsive; and such was the King of Hanover. The story of his behaviour in Germany is such that England cannot be sufficiently thankful that he never disgraced or imperilled her crown.

One class of the community received relief and aid this year, and not before they had suffered terribly. Baring Gould tells us of two villages that were at enmity with each other, and so embittered, that a native of one in peril of his life was asked by a man to whom he appealed for aid, " Be you a Mary Tavey man or a Peter Tavey man ? " " A Peter Tavey man ! Throw me a rope or I shall be drowned." " No, no," answered the other ; " I be a Mary Tavey man, so go on hollerin' till a Peter Tavey man come by," and left the wretch to his fate.

For more than a century this had been the feeling of successive Administrations with regard to the chimney-sweeps ; they were left to their fate as belonging to another caste or tribe. As early as 1817 a Parliamentary Commission had reported that children, stolen or purchased, were compelled to wriggle up narrow sooty chimneys by the most cruel methods. Should they display the slightest reluctance, a wisp of lighted straw was applied to their naked feet, or they were otherwise ill-treated.

Thomas Cooper, in his autobiography, tells us how a sweep offered to purchase him when six years of age for two sovereigns. Cooper's mother, poor woman, looked at the money, which she sorely needed, but,—" I clung tremblingly to her apron and cried, ' Oh, mammy, mammy, don't let the grimy man take me away.' ' No, my dear bairn, he shall not,' she answered; and away we went, leaving the chimney-sweep in a rage, swearing and shouting after my mother that she was a fool, and he was sure to have me sooner or later, for that she could not escape bringing herself and me to the workhouse."

The poor apprentices were compelled to sleep upon the soot, which produced what is known as " sweep's cancer," and the moral degradation of the children was what might be expected from their physical sufferings. In 1834 some feeble attempt at legislative reform was made, but a sufficient number of children had not then been suffocated to justify national interference to the extent required, or the number of victims was not known.

On the 14th of April 1840 a Bill was introduced into the House of Commons which required that no one under sixteen years of age should be bound as an apprentice to the hideous trade, and no one under

C

twenty-one years should be permitted to climb a chimney or flue. Lord Ashley, whose idea of leadership was that held by Sir Charles Napier, who said that every leader should lead by taking a fair share of the work, aided the efforts of the promoters of the beneficent measure, and in doing so furnished details that had been gathered and verified by himself of wrongs inflicted upon children of not more than five years of age. Anxious to neglect no measure likely to ensure success, Lord Ashley endeavoured to secure the co-operation of the Duke of Wellington. The Iron Duke, however, had no pity; he refused his aid, and probably despised Lord Ashley for what he himself esteemed as a weakness.

Lord Ashley, by his eager advocacy of the cause of the suffering and distressed, had earned for himself the intense hatred of many classes. He had been taunted with his exclusive interest in the children employed in the manufacture of textile fabrics, whereas it was alleged that in other factories evils quite as grievous existed. "Give me time; I cannot do everything at once," he had nobly replied. On the 4th of August 1840, after annoying delays, in spite of the Government, he succeeded in securing the appointment of a Commission to inquire into the condition of children not then protected by the Factory Act. He alleged that in the manufacture of tobacco, children of seven years of age were compelled to work for twelve hours per day in a foul offensive atmosphere. In bleaching operations, boys of eleven years, and even younger, toiled often through several nights during the week, and that in an atmosphere of over 120°. In the manufacture of Brussels carpets young children were often aroused at three and four o'clock in the morning, and kept at work for sixteen or eighteen hours, with but little interval for rest and refreshment. In card-setting, infants of five years of age were carried to their work at four o'clock in the morning, and not allowed to leave the mills until eight o'clock at night. The pinmakers were even worse off, for they suffered this additional trouble, that after a certain age they were unfit for their employment, and, vicious and uneducated, had no other means of livelihood open to them than to take to a criminal career.

The House assented to this plea, and the Commission was appointed. This assent, besides being a proof of the growing interest in social questions, showed conclusively that Lord Ashley was obtaining the influence justly due to his character and efforts. In some things, of course, he was vastly in advance of his age, otherwise he would not have been qualified to lead. For example, he himself was an ardent student of prophecy, and believed that the colonisation of Palestine by the Jews would be wise as a measure of policy as well as of justice, and he endeavoured to persuade his father-in-law, Lord Palmerston, to make some initiatory efforts with this end in view.

How amazed and delighted Lord Ashley would have been if he had foreseen that in 1892 no less than 70,000, some say 100,000, Jews would be settled in the land of their fathers, of whom about 40,000 live in Jerusalem itself alone, so that if cities are determined by the majority of their inhabitants, Jerusalem is a Jewish city. A railway from Joppa to Zion is already in progress, and indeed is open through a portion of the district, and other indications of change abound. As yet ignorant of the momentous changes of the future, Lord Ashley went on his way and did his work.

In the December number of the *Quarterly Review* an article upon Infant Labour from Lord Ashley's pen appeared. It repeated the statements he had already made in Parliament with regard to the sufferings of children who were quite unprotected, but it repeated them with no immediate benefit. The year 1841 brought the Melbourne Ministry to an end, an event which was most trying to the Queen, who had come to highly esteem the Prime Minister, whom she understood better than did others, for Lord Melbourne foolishly took pains to appear before the country in a worse light than he deserved. Disraeli, it is true, described him as a " mild middle-aged lounging man, gifted with no ordinary abilities, cultivated with no ordinary care, but the victim of sauntering." The sauntering was a device that deceived no one; it is a pity that it was ever assumed. On the 4th of June Sir Robert

Peel defeated the Ministry, and a general election left them in a worse plight : they were in a minority of seventy-six. The tact of Prince Albert prevented the recurrence of a misunderstanding similar to that which had prevented Sir Robert Peel from taking office two years before. Lord Ashley naturally anticipated that a Cabinet appointment would be offered to him, but he resolved not to accept it if by so doing he were fettered in his philanthropic efforts. Archdeacon Denison once caustically said, that when excavations are made in future years in London, among the bodies of the present generation there will be found " a wonderful amount of cartilage, but very little backbone." The phrase was untrue with regard to Lord Ashley. He could have secured a leading position in the Ministry had he consented to waive his quixotic interest in the poor and outcast, but his resolution never wavered. Knowing that Lord Ashley was inflexible, and would not sacrifice his philanthropy to his party ties, Sir Robert Peel offered him a position at court which was intended to put an end to the agitation the Ministry disliked. " A man is not his own; he must do his duty, and give his whole self to whatsoever it may please God to assign him," said Lord Ashley. " There are paths of profit and honour; there are paths of no gain and humility ; that one alone must be followed where God is a light and a lantern unto our feet," he added, when he declined the office.

The historian of factory legislation appreciated the heroism of this choice, and remarks, "The sacrifice thus made could only be appreciated by those who best understood the pecuniary position of this noble-minded man. He had at that time a large and increasing family, with an income not equal to many of our merchants' and bankers' servants, and a position as the future representative of an ancient and aristocratic family to maintain. By this step, political power, patronage, society, family comforts, nay, everything that was calculated to forward the ease and comfort of himself and in some degree of his family, were laid down at the feet of the factory children of these districts, and freely given up for the sake of the sacred cause of which he had become the leader."

Lord Ashley had the faculty imputed by Mr. Smiles to George Moore, "that of extracting talents from others," and in this ability to rouse others to work to their utmost lay one secret of his success. The following year witnessed one example of this, but before referring to it we must briefly notice another struggle in which he engaged.

The long period of spiritual lethargy had been broken in Scotland by the Disruption movement, and in England by what is generally known as Tractarianism. A number of earnest men carried the Oxford doctrines which had once magnified the crown to another end. For "King" they read "Church," and the ancient loyalty of the University,

once engrossed by the throne, was given to trifles
which they invested with significance, and con-
sequently made of importance.   In the interval
from 1833 to 1841 various tracts had been published which had created a profound sensation in
England.   Shocked by the rationalism imported
from Germany, many people were swept into the
opposite current, and, from disbelieving in what
had sufficient evidence, they placed their faith in
the ritual and doctrines of Rome, for which authority alone was pleaded.   The censure of the Heads
of Houses induced Newman to withdraw from
the leadership of the Ritualists, which headship
passed into the hands of Dr. Pusey, Lord Ashley's
cousin.

Lord Ashley was a firm supporter of the Estab-
lished Church, but he was also before and much
more a Christian and Protestant, and when at
length it seemed possible to do battle with the
Ritualists, he threw himself with ardour into the
contest.   The opportunity arose over the appointment of the Professor of Poetry, a post hallowed
by the sainted Keble, then recently deceased.   Lord
Ashley became chairman of the committee appointed to secure the election of the Protestant, as
opposed to the Ritualistic candidate, and the battle
was fought upon this issue.   Mr. Gladstone naturally ranged himself upon the latter, which proved
to be the losing side.   The sympathies of the
Queen and Prince Albert were warmly with those

who resisted what many people regarded as a subtle form of Romish propagandism.

The Government of Sir Robert Peel was strong and able, and the success of its measures restored the popularity of the crown, which had waned for some years; yet while agreeing with it generally, Lord Ashley often found himself in opposition to it and its policy.

Sir Robert Peel was himself a manufacturer, and the very qualities which enabled him to carry his great financial schemes disqualified him for sympathising with Lord Ashley's reforms. Early in 1842 he avowed himself hostile to the Ten Hours' movement, and the effect was, to quote Lord Ashley's words, that although politicians "feel I am in the right," they will also remember that "Peel is in the Treasury; so the House of Commons will think with *me* and act with *him*."

In May 1842, the report of the Commission appointed at Lord Ashley's suggestion two years before to inquire into the condition of miners was issued. The labour of coal-mining must always be severe, exhausting, and perilous, but the Commission found that males and females were employed together, and many from the age of four or five years.

Little children sat in the cold and dark for hours, their task being to close the ventilating doors after the coal-trucks had passed. These coal-waggons loaded with coal were dragged along the narrow tunnels by women and children, who had to crawl through the wet and darkness in an atmosphere like that of a sewer. Nor was this all, for sometimes girls and women carried huge baskets of coal up a long succession of steps, a slip on which was fatal to one or more of the bearers. The indecency and licentiousness incident to this state of things, and the ignorance and the sufferings of these poor creatures, can be imagined but need not be described.

When the facts were revealed, the country was annoyed and disgusted at the unsuspected evils that had been tolerated so long. Lord Ashley was not the man to imagine that disgust and regret were sufficient; he resolved to attempt at least to remedy what all deplored.

On the 9th of June 1842 he introduced a Bill which enacted, that no lad under fourteen and no female should be employed in the mines; and further, that no engine should be entrusted to any one whose age was less than twenty-one years. The speech which expounded and justified this great measure won for him the approval of the Queen and her husband, the friendship of Cobden, and assistance of Palmerston. To drag such evils to light, to prevent public sympathy from drivelling into sentiment, to compel a legislative remedy, is one of the noblest moral triumphs that ever conferred a benefit upon humanity.

The Government had attempted to suppress the Report, and having failed in that, they passively

resisted the obnoxious Bill.   After he had defeated
them in the Commons, Lord Ashley had great
difficulty in securing a peer bold enough to pilot
the Bill through the Lords, but at length he was
successful, and the measure became law.

In September of the same year, accompanied by
his wife, Lord Ashley made a tour through the
manufacturing districts to see what further reforms
were required.   He felt intensely the misery and
suffering that he was at the time unable to remedy,
but he wisely counselled the factory hands to exercise patience and reliance upon lawful means in
order to procure relief.   His own instincts were
utterly opposed to revolution, and from principle
he could not countenance any outrage upon any
conceivable amount of provocation.   This policy,
while it ultimately secured a lasting triumph, was
best for the sufferers themselves, as it was for the
country.

CHAPTER IV.

FRESH LABOUR ADDED TO OLD SINEWS.

" London ! 'Tis not a city, but a nation,
    Great part of whom are slaves, and ever toil,
Worn out with bitter, hopeless, tribulation,
    Like Israel's sons enchained on Egypt's soil.
Around them seethes with restless undulation
    The tide of life, and in that great turmoil,
        Like cries of those on Moloch's altar bound,
        Their prayers and moans of agony are drowned."

"He often visited those who were not his friends, . . . men of a single idea—money, and how to make the most of it ; men bound up in selfishness, and utterly regardless of the misery of their fellow-creatures. 'I must not be discouraged,' he said ; 'I am doing Christ's work.'"—SMILES ON GEORGE MOORE.

1843–1850.

ECONOMY OF TIME—LOOKING OUT FOR WORK—IN ANOTHER COAT, BUT A SOLDIER STILL—"I CAN'T DO NO MORE"—BETWEEN TWO FIRES — DRAGGING HIS SUPPORTERS THROUGH THE MIRE—NOT IN AT THE DEATH, BUT WEARING THE BRUSH—"GIVE THE CHILD A CHANCE"—"HOW ARE WE TO LIVE ?"

A GREAT worker was once asked how it was that he was able to accomplish so much good. He replied, "By a wise and careful economy of my time." Lord Shaftesbury might truthfully have made the same reply; but one wonders, in contemplating the number and magnitude of his reforms, that they did not weary him. For even good work exhausts, and by its sameness oppresses the mind. The perpetual fund of fresh life that came to him from his daily study of the Bible was probably the secret of his continued vigour and remarkable vitality. Lord Eldon, when he made his first plea, says that he fancied he could feel his little children plucking at his gown and urging him to do his best. Lord Ashley, in addition to the stimulus from heaven derived from the Bible, felt continually the call for help from those who had but few friends to assist them. This year of 1843 witnessed his connection with Ragged Schools, a mission in itself quite sufficient to ennoble a life, but which only shared his heart with other kindred enterprises. But before he undertook this work, Lord Ashley made an attempt to secure some educational advantages for the factory population.

The various Commissions which he had been instrumental in procuring, the information that came to him through his agents and helpers, as well as through his own familiar intercourse with those who worked for their bread, had revealed to Lord Ashley the ignorance in which a vast number of the people lived and died. Kingsley has depicted the condition of the rural districts, and the inhabitants of the towns were little, if any, better.

On the 28th of February 1843 Lord Ashley called attention to this national peril, and moved an address to the Crown. This was agreed to amidst great applause.

The same month witnessed his enlistment in a crusade which has not yet been crowned with victory. Yet it is not too much, after the many victories achieved over equally strong interests, to anticipate that the opium traffic will one day, like the slave trade, be abolished by the free wish of the nation. Lord Ashley's interest in this question was first aroused by Mr. Gurney, who himself was an indefatigable worker in every good and noble cause. On the 4th of April Lord Ashley brought the question before the House in a speech which filled seven columns of the *Times.* Sir Robert Peel, in reply, said that he regarded the opium traffic merely as a branch of revenue, and appealed to Lord Ashley to withdraw the motion. Seeing that he had no chance of succeeding, Lord Ashley agreed to do this; but he had, by bringing the facts before the public, performed his part towards the removal of a burden that still disgraces England.

A more pleasing task awaits us, that of speaking of his connection with Ragged Schools, which fortunate alliance came about by chance. Lord Shaftesbury was in the habit of scanning the papers in order to find opportunities for service as others read them to find chances of gain, and so it fell out that he learned about the Ragged

School movement, which was then very feeble and small.

Rowland Hill appears to have been the founder of Ragged Schools, the first of which was commenced in connection with Surrey Chapel in 1785. A Thomas Cranfield, who had been in the army, and who, after a career of great wickedness, had transferred his energies to the service of a better Master, had in the Mint and Kent Street commenced schools for the degraded class that then swarmed in these now extinct rookeries. Connected with these schools were institutions called Fragment Schools, children attending which were allowed the use of clothes lent them for Sunday's wear. The condition of the poor was awful. The sins of the parents reappeared more vigorous in their children, and so the evil spread. "I does my duty to 'em," said one man slightly superior to his neighbours when spoken to about his children; "I does my duty to 'em. When they does wrong, I wacks 'em. I can't do no more." Few in the poorer districts of London did so much for their children. It was declared upon authority that either more prisons must be built or more schools must be opened.

Lord Shaftesbury went to visit the Ragged School, which was situated in Field Lane, near Holborn Hill. The London City Mission Records furnish a terrible picture of this locality, in which a few poor working men and women were doing what they might under great disadvantages. Lord Ashley

brought new energy and hopefulness to the few
obscure workers that then toiled in the terrible
streets that ran through " the hangman's preserve,"
as it was called; besides stimulus, he gave the
workers what they required to link them into a
band of co-helpers; he formed them into a Union.

A brief trip to the Continent which succeeded
this success was followed by another severe trial,
and that one which to Lord Ashley must have been
peculiarly keen. The factory owners, enraged at his
exposure of the evils of their system, had long taunted
him with the miseries of the agricultural labourers.
They remarked with truth that the labourers upon
his father's estates were ill-fed, under-paid, and
ignorant. But this was no fault of Lord Ashley's,
who, indeed, had no control at all over the estates.
Stung by these unjust remarks, Lord Ashley, at a
meeting held in his county, made a moderate speech
upon the obligations of property and the joy to be
derived from fulfilling them. He spoke plainly about
the evils alleged to exist in Dorsetshire, and urged
an inquiry into the assertions with a view to dis-
prove them or to remove the causes of reproach if
they existed. His father, Lord Shaftesbury, unable
to appreciate the motives that had inspired the
speech, or perhaps condemned by its pleading, was
once more estranged from his son—a somewhat
painful proof that doing right sometimes involves
suffering wrong.

On the 5th of February 1844 the Government

redeemed the promise Lord Ashley had extorted
from them, and introduced a Bill which slightly
shortened the existing hours of labour. But the
operatives, led by Lord Ashley, were not satisfied
with this moderate measure ; they justly demanded
ten hours only. In a splendid speech, in the course
of which he repelled the personal accusations made
against him, Lord Ashley joined issue with the
Government. Mr. Bright replied, and in the course
of a speech, " perhaps the most vindictive towards
the working classes ever heard in Parliament,"
attacked Lord Ashley, and hinted charges which
were at once denied. Lord Ashley demanded an
apology or a frank statement of the alleged offences ;
upon which Mr. Bright declared that what he had
said was the harmless consequence of his own warm
temper, and disclaimed the idea of personal insult.

Sir Robert Peel opposed the Bill, and, with the
purpose of obstructing it, angrily demanded if the
House were prepared to legislate for other industries,
and to his astonishment received an affirmative reply.
He once more remarked that the agricultural labourer
could not be left out; and when this too was met
with a cheer, he exclaimed petulantly that he could
not and would not acquiesce in Lord Ashley's pro-
posal. The House voted against Peel, but by means
of a most unworthy stratagem the Minister obtained
the victory. For when Lord Ashley once more
introduced the Bill, Sir Robert Peel, stirred out of
his usual apathy, declared that if the measure were

carried he would resign, which statement gave him at once a majority of 138 over his opponent. Sir Robert Peel employed the same threat a month later to induce the House to rescind a vote that displeased him, a course which Disraeli described " as dragging his supporters unreasonably through the mire."

In 1845 Lord Ashley succeeded in securing for the children engaged in the calico-printing the small advantages already granted to others by the Factory Acts. During the same year he was again engaged in hostilities with Sir Robert Peel upon the increase of the Maynooth grant, a measure which led to Mr. Gladstone's retirement from the Cabinet. Lord Ashley opposed the smallest endowment of Romanism upon national grounds, holding the views that Mr. Gladstone subsequently avowed in his " Vaticanism," in addition to some even stronger opinions.

On the 6th of June 1845 Lord Ashley introduced his Bill for the better regulation of lunatic asylums and the care and treatment of their unhappy inmates.

In the year 1846 Peel announced his altered views with regard to the corn-laws. Lord Ashley had once shared his leader's opinions as to Protection, but the famine, and perhaps the arguments of Cobden, had led him also to alter his views. But with this difference, that having been elected by agriculturists as a supporter of Protection, Lord

Ashley determined to seek re-election. On the 31st
of January 1845 he resigned his seat, and was not
again chosen by the electors for Dorset, who were
supporters of the corn-laws. Thus it came to pass
that he was not in Parliament when the Ten Hours
Bill, for which he had battled so long and bravely,
was at length passed through the House. He knew
when he placed his seat in jeopardy that this would
probably be the result, but he also knew that he
occupied a prominent position in the religious world,
which he believed justified the sacrifice he made to
conscience. It was in accordance with the extreme
conscientiousness that characterised all his life that
he made this sacrifice, and in estimating his character it ought to be remembered.

Prevented from taking part in the triumph of the
Free Traders and in the struggles of the factory
operatives, Lord Ashley spent his leisure in a careful
visitation of those portions of the metropolis in
which the Ragged School carried on its beneficent
operations.

On the 10th of February 1847 the Ten Hours
Bill was read a second time, and, after a struggle,
carried by a majority of 108. It passed the third
reading in the House of Lords on the 1st of June,
and was received with universal applause throughout
the factory districts. Two apprenticeships had Lord
Ashley served in the interests of the factory operatives, yet he was not permitted to see the reward
of his labours.

The subsequent revival of trade imperilled the law for a time, but the advocates of the classes in question were able to prevent a retrograde movement. In 1850 John Bright, to his shame be it said, seconded a motion which would, if carried, have made the factory working-day extend from half-past five in the morning until half-past eight at night. A compromise was eventually arranged by Lord Ashley, now again in Parliament, and, as fixed by a Bill which became law on the 26th of July 1850, the legal day was declared to be henceforward ten and a half hours for the first five days of the week, while Saturday's labours were ordered to terminate at two o'clock.

On the 31st of July 1847 Lord Ashley returned to Parliament, this time as member for Bath. He had been solicited to stand for that city, and all his expenses had been guaranteed. Without banners or processions, which were then deemed electioneering essentials, he secured a majority of fifty over his antagonist, whose seat had been believed perfectly secure.

The year 1848, which witnessed the downfall of many monarchies believed to be stable, brought trouble to England, but trouble which was to a great extent disarmed of its force by the beneficial legislation which from the time of the Reform Bill until the passing of the Factory Acts had enlisted on the side of order those who alone can accomplish a revolution. The mob are always ready for a riot, but when those who have anything to lose are contented and able to secure the reform of all their grievances by legitimate methods, revolution is impossible. None the less the shock of the earthquake that shook the Continent caused many in England to tremble. The Queen and her husband consulted Lord Ashley, the unportfolioed Minister for the working-classes, as to what they should do to prevent discontent or remove it. He advised a course which the Prince eventually adopted. On the 18th of May 1848 Prince Albert visited St. Giles in state, and presided at a meeting of the Labourers' Friend Society.

Of course, the monarchy cannot rest upon the popularity won by royal carriages with footmen in red liveries, but these pageants are not without their influence, and especially upon those classes whose lives are one long and bitter struggle against disease and want; and as power is rapidly passing into the hands of the democracy, it is especially needful that the Queen should be popular among the working classes.

In many respects Lord Ashley was in advance of his age, and especially so with regard to emigration. The struggle for existence becomes keener every day in our cities; it is almost impossible to supply the necessaries of life to the crowds who throng the courts and slums of London and other centres. General Booth has received almost national support for what, on a smaller scale, others have done before him, but none before Lord Ashley. Taken out of the vicious surroundings which, apart from other influences, would utterly corrupt them, children were given a chance in other and less densely populated lands, where the conditions of existence are less painful. Such a scheme deserves, and should receive, Government assistance; it would certainly be cheaper to do so than to permit them to grow up into criminals, and then to build prisons for them.

This emigration scheme received a new impetus in July of this year, when Lord Ashley attended a Conference of Thieves. He had long taken a profound interest in the work of the London City Mission, one of the noblest of the many societies with which he was associated. One of the agents of this society, whose adventures read like a romance, had won the confidence of the people among whom he laboured. Nearly all these folk were criminals, and that of the worst kind. Moody tells us of a criminal who came to see him, and whose heart was won when the evangelist prayed for him as his brother. This method the missionary adopted, and thieves and burglars came to regard him as their friend, as indeed he was. These thieves had begun to feel the degradation of their life, and forty of them signed a letter which requested Lord Ashley to meet them and give them advice. He consented, and on the 27th of July 1848 this singular interview was held. With the exception of the missionary and Lord Ashley, there was not one among

the four hundred assembled who had not been con-
victed, and some for serious offences. " Several of
the best-known and most experienced thieves were
stationed at the door to prevent the admission of
any but thieves into the room. Some four or five
individuals, who were not at first known, were subjected to a more public examination, and only allowed
to remain on their stating who they were and being
recognised as members of the dishonest fraternity.
The object of this care, as so many of them were in
danger of getting into trouble, as they call it, was
to ascertain whether any who should betray them
were present." [1]

Lord Ashley spoke kindly but plainly to the men,
and counselled them to alter their ways. " But
how," asked one man, " but how are we to live
until our next meeting ? " Another of the company,
in reply to the counsel to pray, answered, " My Lord
and gentlemen of the jury, prayer is very good, but
it won't fill an empty stomach."

George Eliot in her home once put out her hand
to catch a falling vase. The incident furnished
her with a text upon which to discourse about the
instinct which prompts some people to aid the falling. This is indeed a Christian product, and found
in its highest form only among those who fully
accept the Gospel as a working force ; but what is
to be done to lift up those who are injured by the

[1] City Mission Magazine.

fall ? Lord Ashley asked the question, and himself
supplied the answer.

"Will you ever come back to see us again ? "
asked one man.

"Yes, at any time and at any place whenever
you shall send for me," he answered.

Mainly through Lord Ashley's exertions, more
than three hundred of those present were assisted
either to emigrate or to enter upon legitimate employments. This, although a minor phase of his
service, is statesmanship of a high order as well as
practical Christianity ; and Lord Ashley's action is
the more remarkable when we remember how few
there are who do anything at all to alleviate the sufferings or lessen the iniquity of heathen London.

While he was thus seeking to alleviate the miseries
of others, Lord Ashley was not without his share of
that grief which every human life must taste. One
of the bitterest sorrows possible fell upon him on
the 31st of May 1849, when his second son, Francis,
died at Harrow. It was a bereavement that went
deep to the roots of Lord Ashley's nature, and
wrought in him, as such experiences do in all, a
change affecting thought and conduct through all the
remainder of his days. Such experiences alter us
radically ; they test our faith, and show the true
nature of our hold upon other and nobler things.

Because, perhaps, of this consecration by sorrow
to the consolation of those who knew nothing of the
joys he had obtained, Lord Ashley henceforward

gave himself as he had never done before to the philanthropic labours that have become his truest patent of nobility, and which have conferred a rank neither stars nor coronets can impart.

The year 1850 was characterised by the impudent attempt of the Pope to erect a hierarchy in England. It would have been wise perhaps to have ignored the action, which was ill-advised in the Papal interests. It could not affect the stability of the Protestant establishment or succession if the Pope called his servants by one name rather than another; nor could his claim to territorial jurisdiction give him the requisite authority, any more than the title King of France gave the English monarch a revenue from French soil. Lord John Russell, however, saw his chance, and let off one of his famous letters. The squib fired the country, already pervaded with an indefinite sense of alarm. Something had to be done, and a Bill was introduced into Parliament to satisfy the popular frenzy. Lord Ashley, who had the Puritan hatred of Romanism as a system, although he admitted the virtues of many individual Papists, took part in the debate, and on the 18th of March 1851 delivered a vigorous philippic against Popery. An extract may be given from this speech, as it exhibits his conclusions about a system which many, under the influence of Mr. Stead, are beginning to think of more favourably than did their ancestors. "It pretends," he said, " to be spiritual in England, ecclesiastical in Spain ;

it is temporal everywhere though professing it no-
where ; it is democratic in Ireland and despotic in
Austria ; it terrifies statesmen in Sardinia by refusal of the sacraments, and the Government in
France by a refusal to support them at elections.
Here it is in England appealing to the rights of
men and the liberty of conscience ; and there it is
in Italy denouncing them by the lips of Pope
Gregory XVI. as ' that absurd and erroneous maxim
or wild notion that liberty of conscience ought to
be assured and guaranteed to every person.' "

Such plain speaking is a virtue which, when duly
regulated by other and companion graces, is of the
highest importance. Most controversies would lose
their bitterness if the contending factions understood exactly the points at issue.

The Great Exhibition of 1851, which, at first
dreaded as a peril, was afterwards vastly over-rated,
as if it were to somehow put an end to all human
suffering and wrong-doing, involved important work
for Lord Ashley. Two things especially are worthy
of record in connection with his services to the
Exhibition.

The idea that ragged boys might earn a trifle by
blacking shoes was suggested to him, approved of,
and acted upon. Now the Shoe-Black Brigade has
become a recognised institution in our land.

Lord Ashley had become President of the Bible
Society, and in its interest he petitioned for a stand
in the Great Exhibition. This was granted, and

created a precedent for all subsequent exhibitions. The quiet useful work wrought by the Scriptures there sold and distributed will only be known when the consummation of all things arrives.

Another, and that the last Bill he was ever to introduce into the House of Commons, was a measure dealing with lodging-houses. To the vagrant population, composed of broken-down tradesmen, professional men ruined by drink, and the pariahs who inherit a love for mendicancy, such accommodation is a necessity which perhaps in one form or another will always exist.

But the lodging-houses of the past have been infamous dens, training schools for thieves, leaving-houses for burglars—in fact, not only the meeting-place, but also where those who were going wrong were converted into worse and irreclaimable criminals.

In the "Man with the Book," one such resort, called "Teddie's Den," is described with dreadful accuracy. Down in Limehouse and Rotherhithe many such houses still exist, at once a sign and a cause of the squalor and misery around them.

"These places," says Mr. Montague Williams, "which are most numerous in the Shoreditch, Whitechapel, and Commercial Road districts, are simply and solely the hot-beds of crime. They are pernicious in every respect. In the first place, they are the home of the pickpocket and the ordinary street-thief, as distinguished from the burglar. The last named seldom resorts to them."

The Bill introduced by Lord Ashley gave authority to any township numbering 10,000 persons to build model lodging-houses at the expense of the rate-payers. This Act was followed a few days afterwards by an equally beneficial measure, which provided for the inspection of all lodging-houses. These Bills, which he himself conducted through the House of Lords, have proved of great immediate benefit, as well as providing a leverage for legislation which is still imperatively required before some parts of London can be decent, if safe.

On the 2nd of June 1851 Earl Shaftesbury died, and his son, at fifty years of age, succeeded to the earldom and the encumbered estates.

CHAPTER V.

"*THAT'S OUR LORD SHAFTESBURY.*"

> "Sow in the wild waste places,
> Though none thy love may own ;
> God guides the down of the thistle
> The wandering wind hath sown.
> Sow with thine heart in heaven,
> Thy strength thy Master's might,
> Till the wild waste places blossom
> In the warmth of a Saviour's light."
>
> —Anna Shipton.

"It pays to be a thorough Christian. It pays to repent and be converted. It pays to serve Christ. It does not pay in money, but it does in true happiness."—George Moore.

1851–1863.

A PEER, BUT NOT WITHOUT DIFFICULTIES — AT LEISURE FROM HIMSELF TO HELP AND SYMPATHISE—DECLINING A PERSONAL HONOUR—THE BISHOP-MAKER—REPROVED IN PARLIAMENT—BEGINNING TO BE KNOWN—THE WORRY OF DEBT.

WITH his accession to the peerage Lord Ashley (or Lord Shaftesbury as we must henceforth call him) did not terminate his difficulties. It is true he exchanged them, but for others quite as perplexing

60

and worrying; for every man must always wear the
hair-shirt, and his utmost skill can only alter its
colour or conceal it. The evils indicated by the
Free Traders Lord Shaftesbury found really existed
on his estates, and to an extent he had not imagined; he found also other difficulties that he
had not anticipated. Undaunted by a condition
of affairs that he had not expected, Lord Shaftesbury
at once attempted to improve or to alter, as might
be possible.

The farm-labourers, in- whom almost all energy
and intelligence had been extinguished by long-
continued privation, were the first objects of his
care. To lodge them better was his first thought;
then to renovate the village church so as to make
it more suitable for its sacred purpose took more of
his funds than he could spare without economy.
He denied himself the pleasure of living in St.
Giles, and resolved that he would do what he felt
to be his duty before indulging himself.

Nor did the additional cares incident to his new
position induce him to relax his benevolent efforts
for the good of others. He had told the gentry of
Dorsetshire that property involved obligations, and
he resolved, as far as in him lay, to discharge them
to the full. With such assistance as his new
dignity afforded him he increased his philanthropic
efforts on behalf of others. The ingratitude, the
petty annoyances, and the real sufferings that these
labours had involved during the past might well

have justified his taking his ease for a time. But an intense pity for the suffering and lost would not permit him to rest; he was haunted by the remembrance of what he had seen with his own eyes without being able to relieve it.

He said himself that his mind was full of projects, but they were all schemes that purposed the alleviation of human distress or grief. He seemed always at leisure to sympathise and help; and although his original enterprises required all his energies, and that increasingly, he continued to add to them various other claims.

Thus the persecution of the Protestants by the Grand Duke of Tuscany found him ready to plead and labour for them as if no others taxed his resources or filled his hands, and the publication of "Uncle Tom's Cabin" suggested to him an appeal to the women of America to put away the curse of slavery from the Republic.

With regard to the Crimean War, Lord Shaftesbury was strongly with the war party and defended the invasion of the Crimea, with the natural result that all who held different views upon the question about which he spoke viewed him with dislike and enmity. He indeed all his life received his due share of abuse, which all who attempt to drive out the devil may expect and will always obtain.

That some people, at any rate, appreciated his motives was evident when, on the 4th of May 1854, Lord Aberdeen, the Prime Minister, with the con-

currence of the Queen, offered him the Order of the
Garter.   The fear lest his accepting this, the highest
honour of the realm, should somehow impede his
philanthropic work, by binding him to support the
Ministry or induce others to misjudge his motives,
was the chief reason why he refused the coveted
decoration.   At the same time the fees incident to
accepting the ribbon were more than he felt justified
in spending upon a merely personal object.

Another refusal, which was dictated by the same
dominant and supreme sense of duty, involved much
more self-sacrifice.   The mismanagement of the
military authorities in the Crimea had compelled
a change of Ministry, and Lord Palmerston had
become Premier.   He, conscious of the need of
strengthening his Government all round, urged
Lord Shaftesbury, his son-in-law, to join the Cabinet.
Lord Shaftesbury, anxious as he was to aid the
Premier, whose policy he devoutly admired, refused
this request more than once, but, overcome at
length by the entreaties of Lady Shaftesbury and
her mother, he consented to accept office.   But he
did so with the reluctance that most men exhibit to
surrender money or fame ; and with great readiness
he stood aside in favour of another.

But although he had refused rank and pay,
he could not deny the Ministry the benefit of his
sagacity and knowledge of affairs.   During Palmerston's Administration all ecclesiastical appointments
were left to Lord Shaftesbury, who was nicknamed

by the Ritualists the " Bishop-maker." That all who were placed in office by him belonged to the Evangelical School was only what might have been anticipated and cannot be blamed.

One important service that Lord Shaftesbury rendered to the army and nation was the organisation of a Sanitary Commission to visit and render the camp in the Crimea habitable.

All through his life Lord Shaftesbury had been a strong and persistent advocate of doctrines now commonly received, but at one time regarded as fads. Thus he suggested and then completed the arrangements which saved the British army from extinction by disease. In connection with his sanitary achievements he himself once related the following incident.

Lord Shaftesbury once induced an Irish family to permit him to whitewash their room at his own expense. A few days after this operation was finished he visited the house.

" Dear me, what is the matter ? " he asked.

" Well, you see," said the woman, " the wall looked so cold and bare-like that we got the sweep to give it a few warm touches.".

In the year 1855 Lord Shaftesbury called public attention to a relic of the old persecuting days which still disgraced the statute-book. In a land that - boasted of its religious freedom, any city missionary who gathered a few people in a room for such divine worship as suited their capacity was thereby rendered liable to a penalty for so doing. Strange to say, there were found men who actually defended this harsh law, and Lord Shartesbury only with difficulty succeeded in rescinding it.

In the year 1857 a similar trouble arose. Rev. C. H. Spurgeon had licensed Exeter Hall as a place for the celebration of divine worship, in this following the example of Richard Knill, who was, we believe, the first to attempt preaching in a similar building. To the astonishment of some who bewailed the prevalent ignorance, it had been discovered that vast numbers of people, who for various reasons objected to enter churches or chapels, were yet willing to attend religious services held in theatres and halls. Without in the least approving of this feeling, many religious people recognised it, and endeavoured by means of it to influence them for good. It was indeed a case of casting the net where the fish swarmed, rather than of dropping a line where, according to the manuals, they ought to have been. For this movement Lord Shaftesbury had the warmest sympathy ; it had also the approbation of the Bishop of London. A congregation of five thousand people crowded the hall, and half as many were turned away, and these all from the class who were not regular attendants at any form of divine worship. The incumbent of the Strand intervened, and inhibited clergymen from taking any part in the services, which were thenceforward left in the hands of Nonconformists. Lord Shaftesbury thereupon introduced a Bill which purposed permitting any clergyman to take part in special services, with, of course, the sanction of his bishop. This Bill was withdrawn in favour of another which was based upon a compromise that had been arranged by the Archbishop with the High Church leaders, who viewed Lord Shaftesbury's action with dread and aversion, and were therefore certain to reject anything that bore his name.

These services in Exeter Hall proved so successful that some theatres were opened for preaching, largely, we believe, at the expense of the late Mr. Samuel Morley. Lord Shaftesbury, not content with approving, himself often took part in these services—an enormity for which he was once publicly reproved in the House of Lords. This rebuke gave Lord Shaftesbury an excellent opportunity of presenting, in a speech which occupied two or three hours in delivery, a connected history of the movement to the Lords, many of whom were in consequence interested in the services.

In June 1860 the Ragged School teachers of London made a presentation to Lord Shaftesbury. It consisted of an oil painting and a volume, in which was an address subscribed by nearly two thousand people. In accepting this token of regard and esteem, Lord Shaftesbury said, " I would rather be President of the Ragged School Union than have the command of armies or wield the destiny of empires." Some years before he had counselled his helpers in this department thus: "You must keep your Ragged Schools down to one mark; you must keep them, as I have said a hundred times, and, until I carry my point, I shall say a hundred times more, in the mire and the gutter, so long as the mire and gutter exist. So long as this class exists you must keep the schools adapted to their wants, their feelings, their tastes, and their level. I feel that my business lies in the gutter, and have not the least intention to get out of it. And I tell you, my friends, that if, with all the success you have attained, with all the knowledge you have acquired, with all the blessings you have received, you pause in your course any longer than is necessary to take breath, gather strength, survey your position, and thank God—why then, I say, never again come into this hall, for if you do, I will be the first to say to you, as Cromwell said to the House of Commons, 'Out upon you! begone; give place to honester men.'"

This was plain speaking, but it showed the spirit in which he worked for the poor and led the Ragged School teachers, and also the spirit which inspired those who laboured with him and followed his guidance.

On the 4th of the following August (1860) a great meeting was held in the Free Trade Hall, Manchester, in order to present the Countess of Shaftesbury with an address and a marble bust of her husband, the Earl. This gift was intended to be an expression of gratitude that was felt by the factory operatives for him on account of his persistent labours in securing the safe passing of the Ten Hours' Bill. The newspapers of the day gave copious accounts of the gathering, and all of them recorded the graceful speech in which Lady Shaftesbury acknowledged the gratifying gift.

" My good friends," she said, " it will not require many words for me to express the deep and heartfelt gratitude with which I receive the testimonial of your respect and affection. I prize it highly, as coming from a large body of my countrymen, whose character for intelligence and morality qualifies them to estimate at their true value any efforts made for the welfare of the community. You will believe, I am sure, that having watched the progress of your exertions with lively interest, I warmly rejoiced in your success; and it is my fervent prayer to Almighty God that it may be blest through many generations to you and to your children."

Lord Shaftesbury had now lived down most of the calumny and enmity that had vexed his earlier days. A deep sense of his sincerity and worth, as well as a conviction of the value of his public work was now almost universal, and in consequence he became the adviser of others who, like him, desired to help the deserving. By his advice the Holloway Sanitorium and College for Ladies were founded, with great benefit to those for whom they were endowed.

Lord Shaftesbury's statesmanlike views were evident when, on the outbreak of the civil war in America, he urged the claims of India as a source of cotton supply. Without success, he called attention to irrigation as the only method by means of which our great dependency could avoid the periodical famines that prevented it from developing its immense resources and aiding us at home. In this, as in so many other respects, he was in advance of his times, and pointed out the path which others subsequently claimed to have paved through the jungle and morass.

On the 3rd September 1861 death again visited his home, this time carrying away a beloved daughter.

While the smart of this bereavement was still fresh, Lord Palmerston urged and induced Lord Shaftesbury to accept the honour he had declined seven years before, and on the 19th of May 1862 he became a Knight of the Garter.

Trouble of an unexpected kind came to him in 1863, arising, in fact, out of his unsparing care for others. Lord Shaftesbury had left his private affairs too much in the hands of subordinates, with the not singular result that they cared for themselves rather than for his interests. An inquiry into his pecuniary entanglements revealed the fact that he had been considerably wronged, so that, to the worries inseparably incidental to life and his service in it, there was added a worse anxiety arising from a diminished income. It was needful for the per-

fection of his character and the moral roundness
of his example that he should be tried with this
as with other forms of temptation and discipline.
He too must know, as we all must——

> " The sorrow, pain, and weariness
> That make the spirit pure."

Yet he keenly felt the bitter pang and sting that
debt always brings; nor was the fact that he suffered
for the faults of another more than a balm that
little assuaged his pain.   Alas, poor man!

CHAPTER VI.

KNIGHT OF THE GARTER AND COSTER.

"In service that Thy love appoints
 There are no bonds for me,
For my secret heart is taught 'the truth'
 That makes Thy people free,
And a life of self-renouncing love
 Is a life of liberty."

"How to fear God I know not better than by working on at the speciality which He has given us, trusting to Him to make it of use to His creatures, if He needs us, and if He does not, perhaps so much the better for us. He can do His work without our help."
—KINGSLEY.

———————

1864–1881.

THE KNIGHT OF THE INTERROGATION POINT—TRUTH NOT TRUE—LOVE A MAN WHEN YOU LAUGH AT HIM—WHAT IS A COSTER?—THE SOREST GRIEF OF ALL—"PLEASE, SIR, MAY I GIVE YOU A KISS?"—ACKNOWLEDGED AS RIGHT AT LAST.

DR. PIERSON remarks, "It is coming to be a mark of intellectual aristocracy to be sceptical. The first families in the world of intellect have adopted a new coat of arms; their escutcheon is a shield bearing an interrogation point." Which, however

71

true of the age, was certainly not true of Lord Shaftesbury. He held tenaciously to the doctrines usually associated with the term Evangelical, and he combated in the interests of truth both Papacy and Rationalism. Colenso and Pusey were in his view equally wrong, and he warred against them both. The one, he believed, would make the Bible like the telegraphic message received by the Russian general, who found that the Turks had so mixed up the order commanding him to advance on Constantinople that he could not be certain of its exact meaning. The selecting and attempting to reject portions of what was a message from God to be accepted in its entirety called from Lord Shaftesbury as vigorous a protest as did the attempt to place men and ordinances in the throne of God.

Runciman says that you can never love a man unless you are able to laugh at him now and then; which is perhaps true in some senses, but which, as a general rule, is certainly open to question. But the fact that they differed from him upon some points did not prevent friends from loving Lord Shaftesbury very intensely. Yet it must have troubled them, as it did him, when time after time he was compelled to use the sword to defend what the sword had won. Thus only in 1864 did he really secure for the chimney-sweeps' slave-boys the complete protection and liberty which are an Englishman's birthright.

And in spite of all that had been done in the

way of reclamation, it was evident that many of the ragged children of London were still untouched, untaught, and unsaved. On the 14th of February 1866 a meeting of ragged boys was held, when it was found that the majority of those present had been in prison, and that none had any fixed place of abode or employment, and all therefore would of necessity become criminals. Out of the discoveries made at this meeting various useful enterprises originated. The training ships *Chichester* and *Arethusa*, boys and girls' homes at Twickenham and Ealing, and kindred institutions that cannot be enumerated here for lack of space, are among the number. The same year Lord Shaftesbury was again offered Cabinet rank, and that with the Conservatives with whom he politically agreed. But his mind was now fully set upon the great work to which he had dedicated everything, and he declined the honour, which, in spite of his refusal, was more than once pressed upon him. For one thing, the refusal was less difficult because he did not approve of Lord Derby's conduct in first defeating the Whigs by opposing Reform, and then introducing a more drastic Bill of his own. To his mind, such behaviour was not defensible, and he would not accept office with those who were guilty of it. He sometimes mournfully compared his own position to that of "an old tree in a forest half submerged by a mighty flood;" but the parable is not complete or accurate. He was indeed unaffected by the changes evident in religious belief and political practice, but he actively opposed what he considered a flight of locusts coming only to destroy the beauty of life.

In 1872 Lord Shaftesbury became a member of the " coster " fraternity in a manner that may here be briefly related. " Dr. Johnson," says G. H. Pike, "defined a costermonger as a 'person who sells apples.' One of the fraternity, with no reverence for the great Johnson, declares that the definition ' is all gammon.' A coster is a cove wot works werry 'ard for a werry poor livin', and is always a bein 'hinterfered with, and blowed up, and moved hon, and fined and sent to quod by the beaks and bobbies."

Mr. Orsman, whose labours among this class have been described by Mr. Pike, had started a club to enable the costermongers to purchase their own donkeys and barrows. The Earl became a member of this club, and subscribed for a barrow, which was let out to others of the fraternity. And when a local vestry attempted to wrong the costermongers, Lord Shaftesbury interfered to obtain redress for the latter. When this was secured the Earl bade his new friends write to him and again ask for his aid if ever they were in trouble. " Address your letter to me at Grosvenor Square," said he, " and it will probably reach me; but if after my name you put K.G. and Coster, there will be no doubt that I shall get it."

The association of the two titles expressed a truth,

and they explain much of the Earl's popularity. The love of the working-classes for him was intense, because they knew that his interest in them was sincere, and sprang from his love for God and all God's creatures. A certain newspaper proprietor, possessed of much money and but little education, while watching the titled throng crowding his saloon, exclaimed, "'Ow 'orribly 'ollow!" Lord Salisbury never said that about his welcome among the East-Enders of London; he knew that they loved him sincerely, and as much for what he was in himself as what he had done for them. Nor did he care for them alone; for it seemed as if all who were in need claimed and received his sympathy and aid.

An example of this is to be found in his advocacy of the cause of the children employed in brickyards, who had been strangely overlooked when other children were provided for. On the 11th of July 1871 Lord Shaftesbury moved an address calling attention to the fact that nearly thirty thousand children, many of whom were females, were engaged in terrible menial toil for upwards of fourteen hours per day. Nor did he rest until these white slaves enjoyed the protection of the English law.

The year 1872 brought with it a more terrible bereavement than any he had hitherto known. He had struggled manfully against all kinds of obstacles, because he had always been comforted and helped by Lady Shaftesbury. Mrs. Moffat, when she returned to England with her husband, said

with pleasure that she had never held her husband
back from duty; upon which the latter remarked,
" No, indeed; you sent me to work I might have
neglected." Lady Shaftesbury had foregone the
pleasure of her husband's society because she
was one with him in his desire to do good, and
she had sent him forth with new heart for the
terrible toil which had exhausted his life strength.
Now she was to be taken from him, perhaps that he
might exhibit the consolations of the Gospel under
this experience of trouble also.

On the 15th of June 1872 the long forty-four
years of the married life of Lord and Lady Shaftesbury ended for a time, and on the 19th she was
buried. The tribute to her memory in the village
church in which she lies is one of the choicest in
our tongue; it records the writer's reverence for a
" wife as good, as true, and as deeply beloved as
God in His undeserved mercy ever gave to man."

Such examples of hallowed home - life are the
choicest heritage of the nation, and form the most
potent and pleasing form of instruction ever employed by God in building a national love for
virtue. When every couple are linked by love as
pure and tender, England will indeed be " Merrie
England," and not till then.

This sorrow was not without its beneficent effect
upon Lord Shaftesbury, as it can never be when the
grace of God abides in the heart. It impelled him
to new work. In memory of his wife he instituted

a fund whereby the flower-girls of London were enabled to borrow sufficient capital to give them a start in life. A small item truly this Emily Loan Fund, as it was called after the Countess, in the catalogue of the Earl's achievements, but a work the blessed results of which can never be adequately known upon earth. A kind word saved Gough from hopeless ruin, and a trifle may be sufficient to counteract temptation, and save more than one life from utter destruction.

An instance of his kindness was frequently mentioned a few years ago. Lord Shaftesbury himself often related it at the meetings he attended. While moving amongst a crowd of people, a little child took his hand and played with it. It was a little girl, who looked up into the Earl's kindly face and said, " Please, sir, may I give you a kiss ? " He replied, " I am sure you may, my dear, and I will give you one too." Such an act reveals more the character and innate goodness of the man than many vaunted deeds that have won renown.

On the 28th of April 1881 the eightieth birthday of Lord Shaftesbury was celebrated at a great public meeting which was held in the Guildhall, the Lord Mayor of London in the chair. The promoters of the meeting originally intended to hold the gathering at the Mansion House, but it became evident that the Egyptian Hall would be too small to accommodate the numbers likely to be present.

Within the Guildhall Yard the costers with their barrows were waiting to greet their friend, while within the hall itself a number of poor girls from the Flower Girls' Mission strewed the Earl's path up to the dais with flowers.

An address was then presented to him, which was probably more valuable in his eyes because it had been emblazoned by an artist who had been a boy in one of the Ragged Schools. The address was accompanied by a portrait which had been paid for by contributions which ranged from one farthing to a guinea.

The Earl of Aberdeen made a remarkable speech, but, next to Lord Shaftesbury's own discourse, the deepest interest centred in what was said by Mr. W. E. Foster. He recalled the fact that he had, as a Dorsetshire boy, seen Lord Shaftesbury come as a Tory candidate to contest an election. As a manufacturer Mr. Foster had gone North to find the workpeople and their employers at variance and mistrusting each other. He had himself seen the evils complained of, and had laboured with Lord Shaftesbury in removing them; and, said he, " it is well that now, when full of honours and full of years, but still full of power for his great age, he should obtain this testimony and the thanks of his fellow-workers as an encouragement to continuance in energetic and successful work."

CHAPTER VII.

"*EVEN SO, COME, LORD JESUS!*"

"No sickness there !
No weary wasting of the frame away,
    No fearful shrinking from the midnight air,
No dread of summer's bright and fervid ray !
    Care has no home
Within that realm of ceaseless praise and song ;
    Its toiling billows break and melt in foam,
Far from the mansions of the spirit throng."

"Perhaps I shall get training enough to go into the ring before I die ; and if not, I trust one's not going to be idle up there, Tom."—KINGSLEY.

1881–1885.

WELL IN PARTS—"WHAT'S THE GO I' THAT ?"—SOCIAL QUES-
TIONS—"QUIT YOUR LAZINESS"—MY SAVIOUR—GREAT
TALENTS AT GREAT COST DEVOTED TO GREAT PURPOSES
—A NATION CHANGED BY ONE MAN—EYES AND NO EYES.

THE old Scotchwoman who, in reply to an inquiry about her health, replied that she was "weel i' pairts, but ower muckle to be a' weel at one time," implied a truth we are apt to forget. There is always an ailing member of mind or body ; we are seldom in vigorous health in every faculty or limb. But to feel every portion of the body gradually decaying is yet more trying; to bear this well is the severest test of character. Clerk Maxwell, when a boy, inquired concerning almost every act or working of Providence, "What's the go o' that?" But although it is right to ask the question, it is not easy to extract the meaning from every permitted deed of God. Lord Shaftesbury was perhaps spared to grow old gracefully in order that the younger generation might understand somewhat of what we owe to such as he for even common blessings.

To the last he contended vigorously for the sanctity of the Sabbath-day, as essential as much to the political welfare as to the religious prosperity of the nation. For Lord Shaftesbury was not a member of what Carlyle called "The Heaven and Hell Amalgamation Society;" he clearly understood that those who would win heaven must pay the price demanded for it, and surrender much of the pleasure of the present world.

The revelations which came to light in 1883, showing how the unhappy children in circuses, the acrobat apprentices, and others were ill-treated, moved him to urge Parliament to interfere for their protection. But he pleaded in vain; yet if the allegations in a recently published book be true, the case for Parliamentary interference is more than amply made out.

The Luther Commemoration gave Lord Shaftesbury the opportunity he desired of expressing his firm adherence to the doctrines of the Reformation. The vital interests at stake were too important in his eyes to be compromised or imperilled by want of clearness in their defence. He, for one, remembered Goethe's counsel, "Give us your convictions; as for doubts, we have enough of our own."

The publication of Sims's book, "How the Poor Live," and similar appeals, aroused public interest in social questions—an interest which is, we believe, the healthiest symptom of our day. To attend to the urgent need, and to consider what is to be done, is the first stage in every reform; and this men are doing with increasing enthusiasm and force. A Royal Commission, on which the heir-apparent served, examined and reported upon the housing of the poor. Before the Commission Lord Shaftesbury gave evidence.

If in ethics inculcated means to tread in with the heel, this certainly Lord Shaftesbury did for many years, and the introdden seed has not as yet all, or fully, grown.

In the same year of 1884 the consciousness that he would not remain long below prompted the rendering to the veteran such honour as men can confer, which acknowledgment, however, is generally deferred until the capacity for enjoying it has largely gone. On the 5th of March Lord Shaftesbury was entertained at a banquet given in the Mansion

F

House, when three hundred of the leaders of the people assembled to do him honour.

On the 26th of June the City of London conferred upon him its freedom, an honour which would have come more appropriately twenty years before.

Like his friend Spurgeon, Lord Shaftesbury was a " giant for work," and almost up to the closing hours of life he found or made employment for his active mind and willing hands to do. He realised what many now-a-days forget, that it is high praise to be able to say that God never saw one lazy or doing feebly the duty intrusted to him. He knew that not to float with the tide, but to fight one's way through the surf; not to lounge, but to work; in short, to view employment as an endowment, a talent, which, if properly invested, will secure an immense return—this, and this only, is to live. " Quit your meanness," is said to be an American Revival phrase which might well stand with two others, so that the sentence would read, " Quit your meanness; quit your laziness; and quit your selfishness," and those alone who act thus can be truly called men.

For to work gives healthy views of life and kindly sympathy with other kindred labourers. Let us therefore thank God for the opportunity, and thrust our spade into the prairie, which shall one day wave with the harvest that in turn shall yield many a rich sowing, for reapers yet to come.

Lord Shaftesbury was permitted to see his eighty-fourth birthday, and to take part in some of the May meetings of that year of 1884. On the 28th of July he reached Folkestone, whence he passed, on the 1st of October 1884, to that mysterious service of which so little is told us.

The spirit of his waiting days is shown in a saying of his. "I am in the hands of God, the ever-blessed Jehovah," said he; "in His hands alone! Yes, in His keeping, with Him alone."

Before he left London, he had said significantly, "What a comfort it is to know Christ as a personal Saviour!" and, as if in exquisite enjoyment of the privilege, he added, "My Saviour!"

These two concluding words furnish the key to his life and explain his career. To him the Son of God was no mere figure in history, but a vital and present Saviour, sharing his griefs, guiding his thoughts and deeds, and above all transforming his character and preparing heaven for his abode. To appropriate the person, accept the work, and enjoy the society of Christ Jesus made Lord Shaftesbury the man he was, and gave him a spring of life that no drought of unpopularity could affect. Because Christ called him, he was willing to renounce all the pleasures open to one of his rank, to forego all the personal emoluments and fame that were within his reach; to sacrifice his time, money, and friend-ships; to endure calumny, and that from those as true-hearted and sincere as he was himself; and to persist in this course irrespective of the opinions of men, their praises or contempt.

The love that he bore to the Saviour comforted him, while it thus impelled him to heroic sacrifices and vast enterprises that would have been quixotic if they had not been divinely inspired. Because he could say, "My Saviour," Lord Shaftesbury became a saviour to others, sympathising where he could not do more, and doing most when he wept with the sorrow for which none else cared; encouraging others to do their part by doing his own best, and that everywhere and always, and employing the talent that might have secured political office (and that of the highest) to rescue gutter children, and reclaim burglars and thieves; to secure the chance of living decently, soberly, and for the glory of God to the class whom many viewed as scarcely human.

Nor, when we consider the fact that he possessed intellectual abilities of a high order, and could have enjoyed the privilege of teaching by the press, and remember that his speeches were real orations, can we fail to observe the sacrifice of personal ambition to the lofty enterprise to which he had dedicated himself. Hannibal was sworn to undying war with Rome, and Shaftesbury to relentless, unrelaxing combat with all that harmed or troubled the outcast poor of London. His literary abilities, which might have easily won fame, were employed to serve shoeblacks, and the eloquence that might have won the applause of a senate was not indeed

wasted, but nobly employed when consecrated to plead
for those who could not read, but who could reverence, imitate, and love their advocate and friend.

And this sacrifice was happily not made in vain ;
for among the working lives that have called other
activities into play, among those who, because themselves good, have made others labour for the right,
this century has seen none like Lord Shaftesbury.

So the leaders of both political parties, with
neither of which he fully identified himself, agreed
in acknowledging the national obligation to him for
reforms of the most radical and beneficial nature.
" The social reforms of the last century," said the
Duke of Argyll, " have been due mainly to the
influence, character, and perseverance of one man—
Lord Shaftesbury."

" That is, I believe, a very true representation
of the facts," said the Marquis of Salisbury.

Without a doubt Lord Shaftesbury's rank and
natural gifts were important factors in his work,
but they were not the prime cause of his success.
Right away behind all such motives must lie that
which was first taught him by Maria Mills, who,
while instructing a little child, began the moral
revolution which is still preparing the way of God
among men.

In the truth Lord Shaftesbury then grasped
and ever afterwards held fast, in the forces that
then began to act through his own nature, and
chiefly in the Divine Spirit, Who then took posses-

sion of him, we must look for the beginning and fontal cause of all he did of good.

Which remark is important, inasmuch as to us the same possibility is granted. The same Spirit speaks to us, and by our lives may also perform His designs, and that perhaps on a vaster scale than we can imagine.

For the magnitude of the results ought not to go into our estimate, unless we recognise the fact that for a little man to do a little work well is as praiseworthy as when a Shaftesbury fulfils his magnificent mission. James Smetham says, "Then I saw that it is of much more importance to preserve a fresh and tender love to man and to God than to turn the corner of an art career; also, that the opinion of a small circle in a parlour won't be altered supernaturally; that Providence works by natural events, natural opinions and elements, and that the victory which overcomes the world is not that which makes the world succumb, but that which rises above it." Which is the more needful to be remembered because the impossibility of securing human applause or of creating a great opportunity deters many from doing what they might to make the world clearer, brighter, and happier. Great occasions happen rarely, but great possibilities drift past us unobserved. A man noticed that a piece of earthenware curved at either end floated upon a bucket, and he saw in the simple device that which rendered the lifeboat possible. But herein was his greatness, that the trifle which had preached in vain to many that had looked upon it, opened its secrets to him, and to him alone.

All around us are similar parables waiting for the prophet's eye to detect and the prophet's mind to apply their teaching to the needs and wants of the age. The question is, Who will do this work?

Recently one after another many men whose mission has been evident have been taken away from the earth, and although their work will be attempted by those who have loved them, their place in the line will be vacant. What is most urgently required is not so much great leaders, for they will, like Saul, be speedily detected and crowned, so much as that every Israelite should do his own work well in the especial manner and place assigned to him. The rapidly increasing needs and the new perils created by advancing civilisation require all the energy, wisdom, and love that can be brought to bear upon the classes, who require not so much repression as to be lifted up, and inspired with new and adequate motives and incitements to struggle and to win. Those who know they are going wrong, and those who suffer because they have erred, together with the vast horde who do not know what misery they are inducing when they act as their fathers did before them and all their acquaintance behave, these are a sphere for work that might well require not one, but many

Shaftesburys. London alone is appalling, for, in spite of all that has been done and is still being attempted, it is a heathen, and not a Christian, city. And within reach of its misery there are thousands of young men whose ambition is limited to gathering a choice collection of ties and gloves with a side-liking for "dawgs;" who simply do nothing good, and may be regarded of as much importance in the world as the packing that prevents china from breaking. Their presence in the world lessens the shaking and clatter, but the end of all such is to be burned.

To work, and to work simply that others may be benefited, to continue at the task when it has lost its newness and does not appear worth the candle— in short, to work because to do so is right, would, if all believed and acted upon it, revolutionise the world.

And herein lies the secret of happiness; for it is impossible to be free from care or worry unless wholly absorbed in work. The devil does not tempt the busy; when King David was lounging about he gave the chance to his enemy. Nothing. to do always means much to complain about.; the busy alone are the happy. Mr. Howatt tells us of a boy known to him, who on the top of Box Hill rejoiced to himself, humming as he gathered the wild-flowers, "Oh, I do 'joy myself. I 'joy myself now ; I 'joyed myself yesterday, and I shall 'joy myself to-morrow— *Joy*, Joy, JOY !" which words might with truth have been used by Lord Shaftesbury; for, in spite of all he endured, his was a happy life, and his was a happy death. One lesson of his career therefore is that he who would enjoy existence must not seek happiness as a chief end, but must follow the call and bidding of duty.

Upon the whole, we are inclined to place Lord Shaftesbury's claim to honour in the fact that he worked, and that for the worthiest end that ever man had in view. Let it be remembered as one mark of a true noble man that he is a real worker.

Lord Shaftesbury's earnestness, his persistence, his self-restraint, his wide-reaching sympathies, and his inspiring example, indeed his whole life-work, is what might have been anticipated, from the character and power of the principles that had mastered his intellect, secured his affections, and engrossed his ambitions and hopes. In short, his own words, "My Saviour," explain both the marvel of his career and the charm of his character. And if his great endeavour does not compel us to undertake some real work that is not intended for self-improvement but for the comfort of others; if we are not encouraged, having taken up some mission or vocation, to continue in it when unpopular and perhaps painful to ourselves; if we are not driven to seek a commission from the Hand that qualified and set Shaftesbury apart for the apostleship of Helpfulness, to us at least Lord Shaftesbury will have lived in vain.

And in disregarding the obligation that he has thus inculcated, we add to our moral guilt and iniquity. For to laziness and selfishness we shall have added the additional sin of having slighted the influence and call of one of the noblest of God's messengers sent to call men to their duty.

"I have no desire other than to step back from my present place in the world and not to rise to a higher," wrote Dr. Arnold in the last entry made in his journal. "Still there are works which, with God's permission, I would do before the night cometh; especially this great work, if I might be permitted to take part in it. But above all, let me mind my own personal work—to keep myself pure, and zealous, and believing—labouring to do God's will, yet not anxious that it should be done by me rather than by others, if God disapproves of my doing it."

So shall we become

" New moulders of old forms by Nature bred,
    The exhaustless life of manhood's seeds to show;
Let but the ploughshare of portentous times
    Strike deep enough to reach them where they lie."

THE END.

PRINTED BY BALLANTYNE, HANSON AND CO.
EDINBURGH AND LONDON.

Date Loaned

NOV 1952-9	1 mo.		
NS JUN 28 1965	8-13		

Lightning Source UK Ltd.
Milton Keynes UK
UKHW031949010919
348916UK00008B/1777/P